Slithering Snakes
KING Cobras

by Julie Murray

Dash!
LEVELED READERS
1

Dash!
LEVELED READERS

Level 1 – Beginning
Short and simple sentences with familiar words or patterns for children who are beginning to understand how letters and sounds go together.

Level 2 – Emerging
Longer words and sentences with more complex language patterns for readers who are practicing common words and letter sounds.

Level 3 – Transitional
More developed language and vocabulary for readers who are becoming more independent.

abdopublishing.com

Published by Abdo Zoom, a division of ABDO, P.O. Box 398166, Minneapolis, Minnesota 55439.
Copyright © 2018 by Abdo Consulting Group, Inc. International copyrights reserved in all countries.
No part of this book may be reproduced in any form without written permission from the publisher.

Printed in the United States of America, North Mankato, Minnesota.
092017
012018

Photo Credits: Alamy, iStock, Minden Pictures, Science Source, Shutterstock
Production Contributors: Kenny Abdo, Jennie Forsberg, Grace Hansen, John Hansen
Design Contributors: Dorothy Toth, Neil Klinepier

Publisher's Cataloging in Publication Data
Names: Murray, Julie, author.
Title: King Cobras / by Julie Murray.
Description: Minneapolis, Minnesota: Abdo Zoom, 2018. | Series: Slithering snakes |
    Includes online resource and index.
Identifiers: LCCN 2017939224 | ISBN 9781532120749 (lib.bdg.) | ISBN 9781532121869 (ebook) |
    ISBN 9781532122422 (Read-to-Me ebook)
Subjects: LCSH: King Cobras--Juvenile literature. | Snakes--Juvenile literature. | Reptiles--Juvenile
    literature.
Classification: DDC 597.9642--dc23
LC record available at https://lccn.loc.gov/2017939224

Table of Contents

King Cobras 4

More Facts 22

Glossary 23

Index 24

Online Resources 24

King Cobras

King cobras are deadly
snakes. One bite can
kill you!

King cobras are found in Asia. They live in forests near water.

Asia

They are big snakes!
They are 12-15 feet
(3.6-4.5m) long. They
can weigh 20 pounds
(9 kg).

9

They rise up when **threatened**. They spread their necks. They make a hissing sound.

King cobras are green, brown, or black. They have light bands on their bodies. Their bellies are pale yellow.

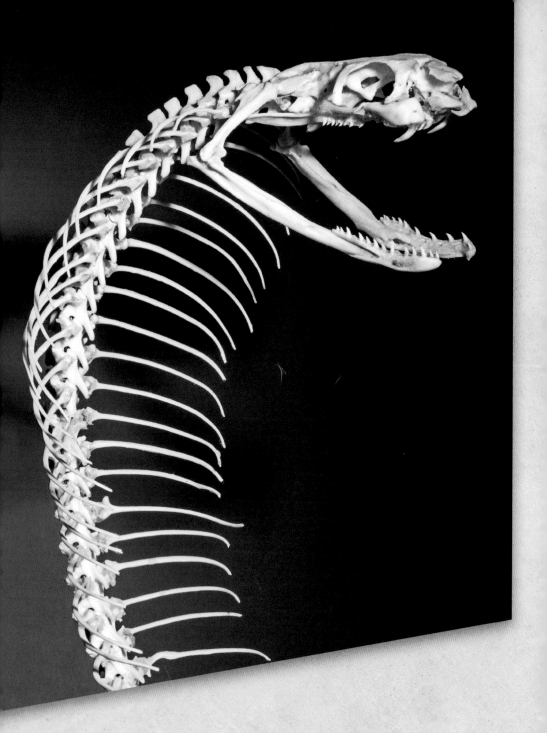

They have sharp **fangs**.

The fangs release deadly **venom**.

King cobras bite their **prey**. They wait for it to die. They swallow it whole.

King cobras mainly
eat other snakes.

They can live for 20 years.

More Facts

- One bite from a king cobra can kill an elephant.

- They are the longest **venomous** snakes in the world.

- They shed their skin 4-6 times a year.

Glossary

fang – a long, pointed tooth that is used to bite prey and inject venom.

prey – an animal that is hunted and eaten by another animal.

threatened – feel unsafe or insecure.

venom – the poison that certain snakes produce.

venomous – poisonous.

Index

Asia 7

bite 5, 17

color 12

fangs 14

food 17, 19

habitat 7

length 8

lifespan 21

neck 11

pattern 12

sounds 11

venom 15

weight 8

Online Resources

Booklinks
NONFICTION NETWORK
FREE! ONLINE NONFICTION RESOURCES

To learn more about king cobras, please visit **abdobooklinks.com**. These links are routinely monitored and updated to provide the most current information available.